THE HISTORY DETECTIVE

INVESTIGATES

Tudor Exploration

Peter Hepplewhite

The History Detective series
Anglo-Saxons
Local History
Roman Britain
Tudor Exploration
Tudor Home
Tudor Medicine
Tudor Theatre
Tudor War
Victorian Crime
Victorian Factory
Victorian School
Victorian Transport

First published in Great Britain in 2005 by Hodder Wayland, an imprint of Hodder Children's Books

This paperback edition published in 2007 by Wayland, an imprint of Hachette Children's Books

Editor: Hayley Leach
Designer: Simon Borrough
Cartoon artwork: Richard Hook
Cross-section artwork (P14): Adam Hook
Map (P7): Peter Bull

British Library Cataloguing in Publication Data

Hepplewhite, Peter
    Tudor Exploration. – (The history detective investigates)
    1.Explorers – England – History – 16th century
    2.Discoveries in geography – English 3. Great Britain –
    History – Tudors, 1485–1603
    I.Title
    942'.05

ISBN 978 0 7502 5294 2

Printed in China

The publishers would like to thank the following for permission to reproduce their pictures:

AKG 8, 9, 23 (left); The Art Archive / Culver Pictures 27 (top); Bridgeman Art Library 17; cover and 20, 21, 24, 25 (left), 25 (right), 28, 29 (left); British Library 4 (left), 5; British Museum 22, 23; Corbis 18, 26, 29 (right); Dennis Cox / China Stock World Views 4 (right); Wayland Picture Library: cover pictures, 13 (top); Mary Evans Picture Library 6, 11, 14; National Maritime Museum 10, 12, 13 (bottom); National Portrait Gallery title page, 16; North Wind Picture Archives 27 (bottom); Yale Center for British Art, Paul Mellon Collection, USA 19.

Contents

Words in **bold** can be found in the glossary on page 30

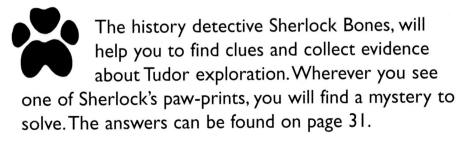

The history detective Sherlock Bones, will help you to find clues and collect evidence about Tudor exploration. Wherever you see one of Sherlock's paw-prints, you will find a mystery to solve. The answers can be found on page 31.

1. What did the early Tudors know about the world?

From 1485 to 1603 England was ruled by the Tudor family, starting with Henry VII (1485–1509) and ending with his grand-daughter, Elizabeth I (1558–1603). Historians call these years Tudor times. During this era, great explorers from Europe sailed round Africa to India and the Far East or across the Atlantic Ocean to America. Their voyages over strange and frightening seas transformed the way Europeans thought about the world.

The centuries before the Tudors are called medieval times, or the Middle Ages. Most medieval people rarely travelled far from home and knew little about the outside world. No-one could go faster than the pace of a horse or a sailing ship, while poor roads, bad weather or robbers often made journeys dangerous.

However, kings, soldiers, traders and pilgrims went on long journeys, sometimes for months or years. Explorers too, trekked overland to exotic places such as Russia, Persia, India and China. Even so, Europeans only knew about a small part of the planet. Africa had not been explored beyond the northern coasts and they had no idea that America or Australia existed.

DETECTIVE WORK

To find out more about the amazing voyages of Admiral Zheng He, go to:

weblinks
www.waylinks.co.uk/
series/HistDetective/
TudExp

If Europeans knew little about the wider world, the Chinese were better informed. In the early 1400s Admiral Zheng He (above) explored India and East Africa. Some historians even think he reached America 72 years before Columbus.

This picture from the Middle Ages shows frightening people who were supposed to live in far off lands.

The Psalter Map was drawn in about 1250. It is called this because it was part of a copy of the Book of Psalms made in the 1200s. It shows a Christian view of the world. The Holy Land where Christ was born is shown at the centre of the map and of the world.

✤ Look at the Psalter Map and see if you can pick out Adam and Eve, the River Nile (look for the large **delta**), the Red Sea and the monsters living in Africa (some without heads).

Men may prove that it is possible to go by ship all round the world. Yet it seems so simple to unlearned men that people may not go to the other side of the earth because they would fall off.

Sir John Mandeville, writing in the 1300s. In Sir John's time many people believed the world was flat and that if someone travelled far enough they would fall off the edge.

Maps made in the Middle Ages show very different ideas about geography and the world, to those maps we have today. The beautiful Psalter Map shown on this page was drawn with the East and the Garden of Eden at the top and Jerusalem at the centre. The earth is divided into three continents with Asia at the top, Africa bottom right and Europe bottom left.

2. How did exploration in Tudor times help people make better maps of the world?

An Indian hurled a bamboo spear into the Captain's face, but he killed him with his lance. When he tried to draw his sword he couldn't because he was wounded in the arm by another spear. When the natives saw that they threw themselves upon him.

Antonio Pigafetta, a sailor who lived to write the story of Magellan's death.

*I*n 1519, five ships with a crew of 260 men set out from Spain. They were led by Ferdinand Magellan. He sailed westwards to Brazil and then south, around the southern tip of South America, into the Pacific Ocean. Three ships pushed on to reach the Philippines, where they were attacked by the natives and Magellan was killed. Only 20 men and one vessel, the *Victoria*, survived the perilous trip round the tip of Africa (the Cape of Good Hope) and returned home to Spain. Even so, it was a triumph. Magellan had shown it was possible to **circumnavigate** the earth.

Caravels like these were often used in early voyages of exploration. They were light, fast and easy to steer. They were only 21 metres long and 6.5 metres wide. A crew of 30 had to live together for months in this tiny space.

As the **charts** of voyages like Magellan's were made public, mapmakers began to record the information. Magellan had proved not only that the earth was round, but that is was far bigger than Europeans had imagined. His discoveries, and the voyages of other

HOW DID EXPLORATION IN TUDOR TIMES HELP PEOPLE MAKE BETTER MAPS OF THE WORLD?

7

→ Magellan 1519–22   → Cabot 1497
→ Da Gama 1497–8   → Columbus' first voyage 1492–3

This map shows the journeys taken by four of the great Tudor explorers.

DETECTIVE WORK

Mapmakers like Geraldus Mercator were trying to draw a 3-dimensional globe on a flat piece of paper. His solution was the famous Mercator Projection. To find out what this was and how it helped sailors to **navigate**, go to:

weblinks
www.waylinks.co.uk/series/
HistDetective/TudExp

great explorers, helped mapmakers to draw more accurate maps of the earth's surface. The invention of printing helped to make maps cheaper and more readily available to ordinary people.

Even the best maps had problems however. They were often inaccurate and out of date as soon as they were made. One reason for this was secrecy. Exploring was very costly and the governments who had paid the bills did not want valuable information leaked to rival countries. Map making could be dangerous too. Geraldus Mercator, one of the best **cartographers** in Europe, was arrested as a spy in 1544. Mercator had travelled widely to acquire information for his maps and this was seen as suspicious behaviour.

✤ Look in an atlas for a map of South America. Find the Magellan Straits. What two pieces of land do the straits pass between?

		Famous Explorers
Date	**Country**	**Voyage**
1488	Portugal	Bartholomew Dias rounds the Cape of Good Hope.
1492–3	Spain	Christopher Columbus hopes to find a route to the Indies but discovers the Caribbean islands.
1497	England	John Cabot hopes to find a route to China but discovers Nova Scotia and Newfoundland in Canada.
1497–8	Portugal	Vasco da Gama sails round Africa to India.
1519	Spain	Hernando Cortes lands in Mexico and conquerors the Aztec empire.
1526	Spain	Francisco Pizarro explores the coast of Peru. In 1531, he attacks and conquers the Inca empire.
1535	France	Jacques Cartier lands in Canada.

3. Why did the Tudors want to go exploring?

The main reason Europeans went exploring was **trade**. Rich people wanted exotic goods like spices, silks and diamonds from China and the lands know as the East Indies. However, the overland route to Europe was controlled by the Ottoman Turks who made traders pay huge taxes on the goods they carried. Most voyages of exploration were looking for an alternative route to the East Indies – by sea.

England was a late starter in this race. The leaders were Spain and Portugal who seemed to be carving up the world between them. North and South America were often refered to as 'the **New World**'. Spanish explorers in America were quickly followed by armies. The Aztec peoples, who lived in what is now Mexico, and the Maya of Central America, were easily conquered and their lands became Spanish **colonies**. Soon fabulous treasure fleets were heading back to Spain loaded with looted silver and gold. At the same time, the Portuguese set up forts along the coast of Africa to protect their sea routes to Asia and stop rivals stealing their trade.

This Aztec picture shows their warriors fighting Spanish soldiers in 1519. When the Spanish invaded, 20 million native people lived in Mexico. A century later – war starvation and disease had reduced their numbers to less than one million.

✤ What weapons can you see in the Aztec picture? What is the 'secret weapon' being used by the Spanish?

King Henry VII was interested in finding an English route to the Indies and paid John Cabot to go exploring in 1497–8. The results were poor. Cabot landed in the country we now call Canada and returned without discovering any fabulous cities, gold or spices. On his second voyage his ship disappeared and he was never heard of again.

We must take as our example the Kings of Spain and Portugal, who have not only enlarged their empires, greatly enriched themselves and their subjects, but have also trebled the numbers of their ships and sailors. It is certain that the strength of our country depends upon the number of ships and sailors we possess.

Richard Hakluyt (pronounced hak-let) an English geographer writing in 1589

The Royal Exchange, London, 1600, where merchants met and traded their goods. Some enterprising English merchants set up companies to pay for early voyages of exploration. In return the government promised that they could control any trade with new lands they found.

King Henry VIII had no interest in exploration and it was another 50 years before England sent out expeditions again. In 1553, English explorer Richard Chancellor sailed into the Russian White Sea and travelled 2,400 kilometres to Moscow. He was able to set up trading agreements with the Russian Tsar (King), Ivan the Terrible.

By the 1550s English merchants watched with envy as the riches of the Americas were carried off by the Spanish. They wanted a slice of the action too. England was soon to become a major rival to Spain and this led to war.

4. Why did religion make people want to explore?

The great sea Battle of Lepanto was fought in the Ionian Sea in 1571. A Christian fleet led by Spain defeated the Turkish fleet and saved Europe from **invasion**. The Spanish were furious that Queen Elizabeth I, a Christian Queen, allowed sailors like Sir Francis Drake to attack their ships while they were fighting the Muslim Turks.

A second important reason for exploring the world was religion. In early Tudor times all Europeans were Christians and they feared the growing might of the Ottoman Turks, who were **Muslims**. The Turks had captured the great city of Constantinople, now known as Istanbul, in 1453 and ruled most of the Middle East. By 1520, the Turkish fleet was the most powerful in the Mediterranean Sea.

European monarchs wanted to spread the Christian faith to new lands before Muslim explorers reached them first. Christopher Columbus took the first **missionaries** to America in 1493. Among the 1500 settlers, he carried five *religiosos* who had the special job of converting the people of the **New World** to Christianity.

By the 1530s, however, Christians were arguing among themselves about religion. Most Western Europeans had been **Catholics** for centuries and followed the leadership of the Pope in Rome. However, a growing minority of people were becoming **Protestants**. This meant they had turned away from the teachings of the Catholic Church.

When the Pope refused to give King Henry VIII a divorce from his Spanish wife, Catherine of Aragon, Henry made England a Protestant country. During the reign of Elizabeth I, England was at war with Spain, the most powerful Catholic country from 1585 to 1604. During these years the English tried to set up Protestant settlements in North America to challenge Spanish control of Mexico and South America.

✵ Find the capital city of Turkey, Istanbul, in a world atlas. Istanbul was the Christian city of Constantinople until the Turks captured it in 1453. Look at the map. Why do you think Constantinople was called the gateway to Europe?

Indian boats came alongside our ship and took one of our men to the nearby city of Calcut…The first greeting he was given was: 'May the Devil take you! What brought you here?' They asked what he wanted so far from home and he told them that we had come in search of Christians and spices.

Portuguese explorer Vasco da Gama's account of his trip across the Indian Ocean. His ships reached India in May 1498. This was the first crossing of the Indian Ocean by a European.

Turkish pirates even raided parts of England and English ships in search of loot and white slaves. Using fast galleys they attacked British shipping at will.

DETECTIVE WORK

To find out how the Reverend Devereux Spratt was carried off by Muslim pirates in the Irish Sea, go to:

weblinks

www.waylinks.co.uk/series/
HistDetective/TudExp

5. How did Tudor explorers find their way?

Navigating, or finding your way at sea, was difficult in Tudor times. Many unlucky ships were wrecked on hidden rocks. Some drifted far from land until the crew died of thirst. Others were captured or sunk when they sailed into enemy waters. Accurate navigation was the key to staying alive.

Most Tudor seafarers only sailed on short sea routes near the coast. On a clear day they could find their way fairly easily by using landmarks such as hills, bays or church steeples. Explorers, however, faced the perils of the open sea. They might be out of sight of land for months and relied on what they called 'dead reckoning'.

This was done by the navigator, who, next to the Captain, was the most important member of the crew. To make an estimate of their position he had to know the speed of the ship, the direction of travel and how long the ship had travelled in that direction.

To work out the direction of travel, the navigator looked at a compass. To work out the speed he used a 'log line'. This was a log fastened to a piece of rope with knots tied in it, at equal distances apart. The log was thrown overboard and, as the ship moved away, he counted how many knots were let out in a set time. Since Tudor times the speed of ships has been measured in knots.

A sixteenth century sailor's compass.

Finally, to calculate the length of time travelled in a given direction, the navigator used hourglasses filled with fine sand, like big household egg-timers. Every ship carried a large glass that ran for four hours and a smaller glass that ran for half an hour. The large glass was also used to time the six four-hour shifts worked by sailors – known as 'watches'. The smaller glass was used to split each 'watch' into eight equal periods known as 'bells'.

Dead reckoning was not very accurate because it did not allow for errors caused by winds and sea currents. Christopher Columbus, however, was very good at this tricky art. On his return from his second voyage to America in 1496 he found land only 56km away from where he calculated it should be. And that was after six weeks sailing a zigzag course across the Atlantic Ocean!

A sixteenth century hourglass.

☙ Hourglasses were not very accurate. What might stop them working properly?

Sailors could calculate their line of latitude (how far north or south they were) using an astrolabe. This was used to measure the height of the sun or the pole star above the horizon.

6. What was life like on board a Tudor ship?

Life for Tudor sailors was hard. Ships were tiny and packed with stores for long voyages such as spare sails, ropes, firewood, food, water and weapons. The officers had their own quarters but the men had to sleep where they could, on the gun deck, among the supplies or in the open.

Each day began with prayers, when the sailors asked to be returned safely. For work, the men were divided into two groups called watches (see page 13). Jobs included pumping out water, repairing sails, scrubbing decks and preparing food. Sailors who disobeyed an order were flogged, while thieves were dunked in the sea, often until they were nearly drowned.

In violent storms sailors might be washed overboard or the ships driven onto rocks and wrecked.

The biscuit was so full of worms that, God help me, I saw many wait till nightfall to eat the porridge made of it so as not to see the worms.

Ferdinand, son of Christopher Columbus, on his father's voyage to America.

It rotted all my gums, which gave out a black and putrid blood. My thighs and lower legs were black, and I was forced to use my knife each day to cut into the flesh, to release this black and foul blood.

A sailor in the fifteenth century describing what is was like to have scurvy.

At first there was fresh food to eat, while animals were kept on board for meat. After a few weeks however, the crew had to eat preserved foods: salted beef and pork, dried cod and dried peas. Dried bread was called 'ship's biscuit' because it was baked hard enough to last as long as 50 years – if the **weevils** didn't get it first!

Poor food led to the death of many sailors from an illness called scurvy, caused by a lack of vitamin C. Bad hygiene led to outbreaks of typhus and dysentery. Explorers lost more men to disease than to storms or fighting.

✿ Christopher Columbus discovered an amazing space saving bed for sailors. What do you think it was?

DETECTIVE WORK

Tudor sailors took ship's biscuits with them on long voyages, because they lasted longer than bread. Try this recipe and make your own. Make sure you ask an adult to help you.

Ingredients
250g of coarse wholemeal flour (stone ground if you can get it)
5g of salt
Method
1. Mix all the ingredients with a little water to make a stiff dough.
2. Leave for $\frac{1}{2}$ hour and then roll out very thickly.
3. Separate into three or four biscuits.
4. Bake in a hot oven at approximately 220°C, or gas mark 7, for 30 minutes.
5. Leave the biscuits in a warm dry atmosphere to harden and dry out.

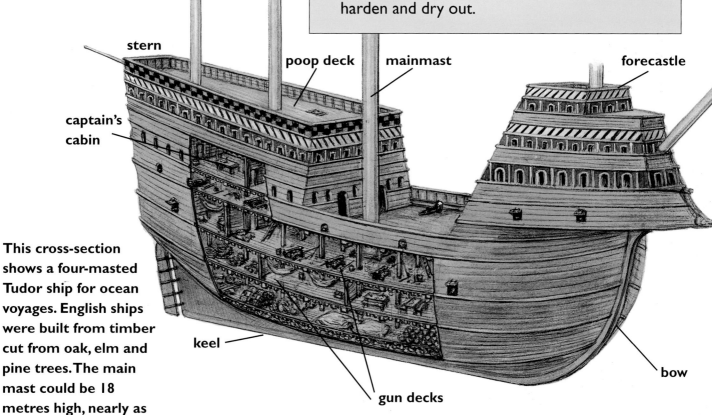

stern   poop deck   mainmast   forecastle

captain's cabin

keel

gun decks

bow

This cross-section shows a four-masted Tudor ship for ocean voyages. English ships were built from timber cut from oak, elm and pine trees. The main mast could be 18 metres high, nearly as long as the ship itself.

7. Why did Sir Francis Drake sail around the world?

Sir Francis Drake was one of England's most famous sailors and a favourite of Queen Elizabeth I. In 1577, she chose him for a top-secret mission – to be the first Englishman to sail around the world. His experience made him the ideal choice.

Francis Drake was born around 1541– 43 into a poor Devon family. He learned his trade as a seaman working for his kinsman, John Hawkins. Between 1562– 65 they made two voyages to Africa to capture slaves and then sailed to the West Indies to sell them to Spanish settlements. Later, Drake made a fortune by attacking Spanish treasure ships sailing home from South America. Queen Elizabeth called him her 'little pirate' and in return for her share of the loot made him a **buccaneer**.

🐾 Look at the portrait of Francis Drake. Why do you think the artist has painted him with his hand on the globe?

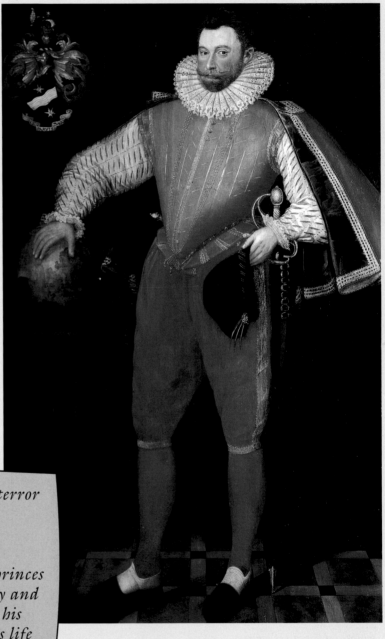

Portrait (c.1580) of **Sir Francis Drake** showing him in his finest clothes after his voyage round the world. The sword shows that he is a gentleman. This was important to Drake: it meant that in spite of his humble background he had made a success of his life.

His name was a terror to the French, Spaniard and Portuguese and ***Indians****. Many princes of Italy, Germany and elsewhere wanted his picture during his life time, enemies as well as friends.*

Historian Edmund Howes, in his *Chronicles*, 1615

Drake set sail on his mysterious voyage from Plymouth on 13 December 1577. Even the crew were not told where they were going until they reached South America. He led a small fleet of five well-armed vessels and some 170 men. His own ship was called the *Pelican*. It weighed just 100 tonnes, carried 18 guns and was only 23 metres long.

Drake's orders were to sail round the dreaded Cape Horn and into the Pacific Ocean, exploring the western coastline of the **New World**. England was not at war with Spain but he was expected to rob as many Spanish ports and ships as he could. No-one knows the full details of Drake's orders, but it is likely he was told to look for sites for English **colonies** and new **trade** routes to Asia.

A sixteenth century engraving of a Spanish treasure ship being attacked by Drake and his men. They took any treasure, but usually let the ship sail home.

8. What adventures did Drake have sailing round the world?

Drake renamed the *Pelican*, the *Golden Hinde*, after he sailed round Cape Horn into the Pacific. This picture shows a modern reconstruction of Drake's famous ship.

Drake's voyage faced disaster several times, but it began with a stroke of luck. Off the coast of North Africa, Drake captured a Portuguese merchant ship and forced the navigator, Nuno de Silva, to be his pilot. De Silva had far better **charts** of South America than the English. Even so, the passage to Cape Horn was long and wearing. Drake fell out with one of his captains, Thomas Doughty. He accused him of stirring up bad feelings among the men. Doughty was put on trial for **mutiny** and beheaded on 20 June 1578.

Three ships pushed on through the Straits of Magellan and into the Pacific. Here, the *Marigold* was sunk in a storm while the *Elizabeth* was forced to turn back. Drake and a crew of just 58 headed north alone aboard the *Pelican*. The next weeks, brought plunder aplenty. Spanish settlements in Chile and Peru were undefended and easy prey. The greatest prize was the treasure ship *Cacafuego*, which was loaded with gold and silver.

I must have the gentlemen to haul and draw with the mariner, and the mariner with the gentlemen. Let us show ourselves to be of a company and let us not give occasion to the enemy to rejoice at our decay and overthrow.

Part of a rousing speech made by Drake after the execution of Doughty. He wanted to pull his men together before they sailed into the Pacific.

Drake continued north as far as the modern American state of Washington, looking in vain for the fabled **North West Passage** back to the Atlantic. Turning south again he landed somewhere in what is now California. Drake called the area 'Nova Albion' and claimed it for Queen Elizabeth. From there he sailed across the Pacific to the Moluccas and took six tonnes of **cloves** on board. He returned to Plymouth on 26 September 1580.

DETECTIVE WORK

Spanish mothers would frighten naughty children by telling them that Drake would come and get them if they didn't behave. To find out about Drake's great raid on Spain in 1587 and how he singed 'the King of Spain's beard', go to:

weblinks
www.waylinks.co.uk/series/HistDetective/TudExp

This map shows Drake's famous voyage. He helped to make an accurate picture of the geography of the world. When his ships were driven south by a storm off Cape Horn he made one crucial discovery. Tierra del Fuego was not part of a vast southern continent but just a group of islands.

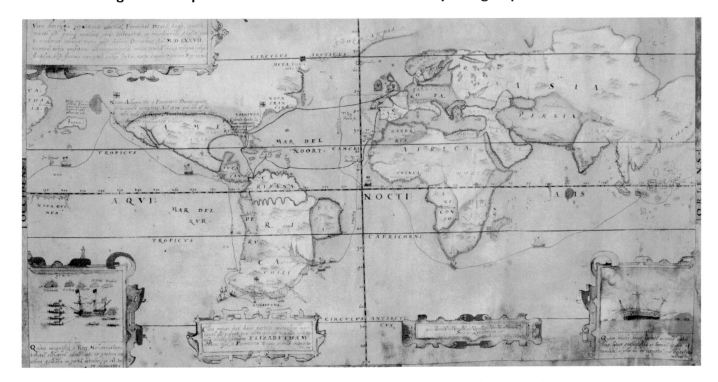

✿ Which part of Drake's voyage around the world is not shown on this 16th century map? (Hint: look at North America.)

9. Why did Sir Walter Raleigh set up a colony at Roanoke?

Sir Walter Raleigh was another favourite of Queen Elizabeth I. Young, dashing and handsome he was also an able soldier, sailor, poet and writer. In 1580, he went to Ireland where he put down a rebellion against English rule. Impressed by his talents, Elizabeth knighted Raleigh and rewarded him with grants of land.

Raleigh was inspired by his half brother, Sir Humphrey Gilbert, to set up **colonies** in North America. In 1583, Gilbert had explored Newfoundland to look for a good site for a settlement, but his ship was lost at sea on the way home. The following year, Raleigh found enough **backers** to make a second attempt.

The idea proved popular for different reasons. Merchants wanted to **trade** English goods, like woollen cloth, to the natives. Churchmen hoped to gain new converts to the **Protestant** faith, while leading sailors wanted to build naval bases to stop the Spanish taking over all of the **New World**. Not least, likely settlers planned to make better lives for themselves and their families.

Sir Walter Raleigh (c.1552–1618) was born in Devon, like Sir Francis Drake. Although he was from a rich and noble family, he spoke in a broad Devon accent. He spelt his name 'Ralegh' not Raleigh.

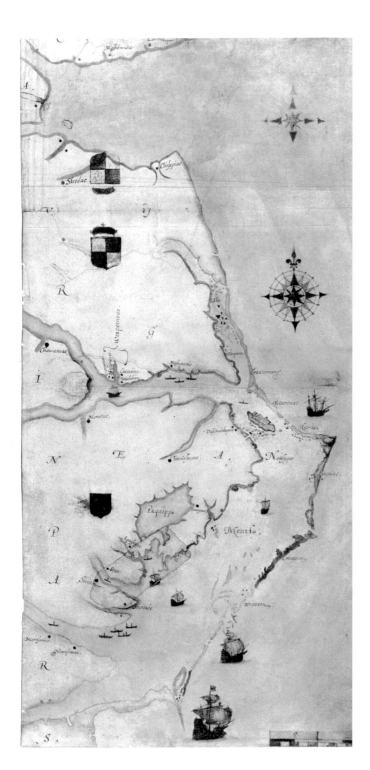

This map of the Roanoke area was drawn by John White, the artist who went with the Roanoke settlers. His beautiful water colours are one of the best sources of information about the colony.

In 1584, Raleigh sent a scouting expedition to America to find a good place to settle. The scouts discovered an island called Roanoke off the coast of modern North Carolina. They reported that the native people were 'gentle' and that the land was 'most pleasant and fertile'. Encouraged by this, in 1581, Raleigh shipped out 500 men, most of them soldiers. Ralph Lane, a noble and army officer, was in charge of the **colony**.

This Island had many goodly woods full of Deer, Conies [rabbits], Hares, and Fowl... The soil is the most plentiful, sweet, fruitful and wholesome of all the world...After two or three days the King's brother came aboard the ships and drank wine, and did eat of our meat and of our bread, and liked exceedingly thereof...They offered us good exchange for our hatchets, and axes, and for knives, and would have given anything for swords: but we would not part with any.

Written by Captain Arthur Barlowe, who discovered Roanoke for Walter Raleigh in 1584.

DETECTIVE WORK

Fort Raleigh on Roanoke Island is now a top tourist destination in the USA. To find out more about the fort, go to:

weblinks

www.waylinks.co.uk/series/HistDetective/TudExp

10. What happened to the Roanoke colony?

At first, the settlers were welcomed by the local Algonquin **Indians** but soon fighting broke out. During the first bitter winter, food was scarce and the English began to steal from the native Indians to save themselves from starving. Vital supplies from England did not arrive on time and in 1586 the settlers gratefully accepted the offer of a passage home from Francis Drake.

In 1587, Walter Raleigh tried again. This time he sent just 110 people, including 17 women and nine children. To try and avoid fighting with the Indians there were no soldiers. Raleigh gave the new colony the grand name of the 'Cittie (City) of Ralegh'. The governor was John White (see page 21), the artist.

Problems began on the journey out. The settlers were supposed to pick up supplies of salt and fruit at Haiti but the sailors spent the time attacking Spanish ships. At Roanoke, the Indians were hostile and attempts to make peace went badly wrong. The settlers attacked a village of friendly natives by mistake. Only the support of one Indian chief, Manteo, stopped them being wiped out.

> *28 July: George Howe was killed by the savages who came to Roanoke to spy on us or to hunt. They found him wading in the water alone…He was shot with sixteen arrows and then killed with wooden swords. After this they beat his head into pieces.*
>
> Diary of John White, 1587

❀ Why do you think Raleigh sent families on the second attempt to set up a colony at Roanoke?

Algonquin Indians fishing with traps and spears, painted by John White. The Indians greeted the first group of colonists kindly and showed them how to fish and which local herbs were good for medicine.

In August 1588, John White was forced to return to England to get more supplies – and bad luck struck again. War with Spain meant there were no ships to spare and it was not until August 1590 that he got back to America. To his horror he found the colony deserted. There was no sign of fighting and the settlers seemed to have left in a hurry.

The only clue was the word CROATAN, the name of a nearby island carved on a post. Storms prevented John White from sailing to Croatan to look for the Roanoke settlers. He returned to England and never found his family.

The fate of the settlers at Roanoke remains a mystery, but it is likely they were attacked by Indians like the warrior in this picture.

The Spanish Armada, the invasion fleet sent by King Philip of Spain to conquer England. John White was not allowed to take supplies back to Roanoke until the threat from Spain had passed. He had left his daughter and tiny granddaughter, the first English child born in America, behind. He never saw them again.

12. How did English settlement affect Native Americans?

In March 1622 hundreds of Powhatan Indians attacked the Jamestown Settlement and killed around 350 people. The English hit back in the coming years and almost wiped out the Powhatans.

The settlement at Roanoke was a failure, but soon the English were back. The first successful colony was founded at Jamestown, Virginia in 1607 and the second at Plymouth, in what is now Massachusetts, in 1620. This was the beginning of a long **invasion** that was to destroy the way of life of the Native Americans.

Where today are the Pequot...the Mohican, the Pokanoket, and many other once powerful tribes? They have vanished before the greed and cruelty of the White Man, as snow before a summer sun.

Tecumseh of the Shawnees, 1812

The story of Pocahontas could have been a warning to the Native Americans about their future. During the first months of the Jamestown colony the leader, Captain John Smith, led armed patrols to take food from the Powhatan **Indians**. When Smith was captured, Pocahontas, the 13 year old daughter of Chief Wahunsonacook, begged for his life. Grudgingly her father agreed and the Indians began to **trade** with the English. This saved the colony from starvation.

As more settlers arrived, trouble flared. The English burnt Indian villages, and murdered the children of local chiefs. In 1613, Pocahontas was taken prisoner by the settlers and taught to behave like an English woman. She was baptised as a Christian and married a settler, John Rolfe.

An engraving of Pocahontas dressed in European clothes when she visited England in 1616.

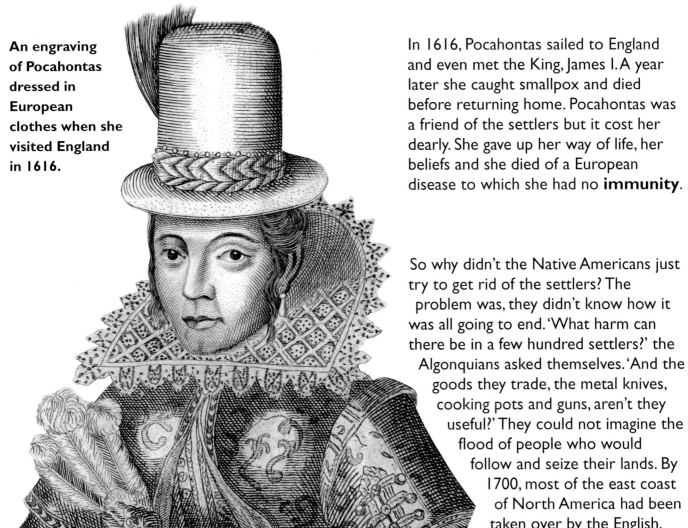

In 1616, Pocahontas sailed to England and even met the King, James I. A year later she caught smallpox and died before returning home. Pocahontas was a friend of the settlers but it cost her dearly. She gave up her way of life, her beliefs and she died of a European disease to which she had no **immunity**.

So why didn't the Native Americans just try to get rid of the settlers? The problem was, they didn't know how it was all going to end. 'What harm can there be in a few hundred settlers?' the Algonquians asked themselves. 'And the goods they trade, the metal knives, cooking pots and guns, aren't they useful?' They could not imagine the flood of people who would follow and seize their lands. By 1700, most of the east coast of North America had been taken over by the English.

Diseases like smallpox and measles were like a European secret weapon. They killed many Native Americans, often leaving tribes too weak to fight.

DETECTIVE WORK

Tecumseh was a great Indian leader in the early 1800s. Find out how close he came to stopping the invasion of the White Men.

13. Your project

*I*t's amazing how far Tudor discoveries still affect our everyday lives. To find out how, you needn't travel further than your kitchen cupboards. Tudor explorers brought back some of our tastiest foods from the **New World**, such as: maize (sweet-corn), chocolate, tomatoes, potatoes, peanuts, pumpkins, squash, sweet and chilli peppers, and turkey.

The technique used by
Florida Indians to plant maize
in the sixteenth century.

Choose a food from the list on the left and try to find out:

- How Native Americans grew, cooked and ate the food?
- Did they use it for anything else? (You'll be surprised what can be made from corn husks.)
- Which explorer found the food and what did they think about it? (Not many Europeans liked chocolate at first, why not?)
- When was the food first taken back to Europe and to England? (Why was chocolate a top secret in Spain?)
- How has the food changed over the centuries? (What colour were the first tomatoes? Hint: it probably wasn't red.)

Project Presentation

- Research your food. Ask a librarian to show you some good books, for example: *The Potato: How the Humble Spud Rescued the Western World* by Larry Zuckerman.
- Use the Internet. Put phrases like 'food from the New World' or 'the history of cocoa' into a search engine.
- Find out if there is a society, museum or historic site connected to your food e.g. look up the website of the Potato Fan Club.
- Cut out or download pictures showing the history of your food. You could use them to make a short Power Point presentation.

Ripe cocoa pods.

A Mexican Indian preparing chocolate in 1553.

Sherlock Bones has been finding out about tobacco, another plant from America. When Christopher Columbus arrived in Cuba in 1492, he saw natives smoking rolled tobacco leaves.

The first man to bring tobacco to Europe was a monk, Ramone Pane, who went with Columbus on his second trip to America. Do you remember the husband of Pocahontas, John Rolfe? He grew one of the first commercial crops of tobacco in 1612, in Virginia.

Glossary

backer A person who provides money or support for a project.

buccaneer A sailor who behaved like a pirate but who worked with the approval of the king or queen.

cartographer A mapmaker.

Catholic A member of the Roman Catholic Church led by the Pope in Rome.

charts Maps made by explorers of their voyages.

circumnavigate To sail round the world.

cloves A valuable spice.

colonies Land conquered, ruled over or settled by another country.

culture Way of life.

delta Place where a river splits into smaller water ways.

East Indies India and other lands in the Far East like modern Indonesia.

empire Lands settled or conquered by the people of another country.

Indian A Native American mistakenly called an Indian by European explorers, who thought they had reached India.

immunity Resistance to disease.

Incas The native people of Peru conquered by Pizarro.

invasion Attack on another country.

missionaries Priests trained to spread the Christian religion in a foreign country.

Muslim A person who believes in the Islamic religion founded by the prophet Mohammed.

mutiny A rebellion against the commanding officer of a ship.

navigate To find the right direction during a journey.

North West Passage For centuries British explorers believed it was possible to sail around the top of North America to reach the Pacific.

New World The name given to the continents we now call North and South America.

palisades Large stakes.

plunder Stolen treasure.

Protestant A Christian who had turned away from the teaching of the Catholic Church.

religiosos Missionaries or special priests to spread the Catholic faith.

supreme being A great spirit or all-powerful god.

weevils Insects that lived in ship's biscuits.

wigwams Huts made from bark or skins used by Algonquian Indians.

trade Buying and selling goods to make a profit.

Further Information

Books to Read

The History Detective Investigates: Tudor War by Peter Hepplewhite (Wayland, 2003)

Sir Francis Drake by Neil Champion (Heineman, 2001)

1492 The World Five Hundred Years Ago by Deborah Manley and Dr Geoffrey Scammell (Guiness, 1992)

People in the Past: Tudor Explorers by Haydn Middleton (Heinemann, 2004)

Look Inside: A Tudor Warship by Brian Moses (Wayland, 2002)

Places to Visit

The Golden Hinde
St Mary Overie Dock, Cathedral Street,
London SE1 9DE
www.goldenhinde.org

The National Maritime Museum
Greenwich, London
www.nmm.ac.uk

Buckland Abbey (The home of Francis Drake)
Yelverton, Devon

Answers

Page 5 ❈ Adam and Eve are the faces in the circle below the picture of Jesus, the River Nile runs down the right side of the world to the big delta, the Red Sea is bright red and the monsters are the tiny figures on the right side of the world.

Page 7 ❈ The Strait of Magellan is the passage between mainland South America, Tierra del Feugo and Cape Horn to the south. It is the biggest natural passage between the Atlantic and Pacific Oceans.

Page 8 ❈ The Spanish and the Aztecs are armed with shields, swords and a lance. The 'secret weapon' was horses. The Aztecs had not seen horses before and did not know how to fight mounted soldiers.

Page 11 ❈ Constantinople controlled the Bosphorus, the narrow straits between Asia and Europe. An army invading Europe from Asia had to capture or go round Constantinople.

Page 13 ❈ The consistency of the sand could affect its rate of flow, as could condensation in the glass.

Page 14 ❈ Columbus found people in the West Indies sleeping in hammocks. They quickly became popular in ships and were far more comfortable than sleeping on decks.

Page 16 ❈ This portrait was painted in the 1580s when Drake was a national hero. His hand spans the globe from one side to the other, showing his success in sailing round the world.

Page 19 ❈ The long trip north to modern Washington State and back to 'Nova Albion', modern California.

Page 23 ❈ Families would have more children and this would give them greater reason to make the colony work.

Page 25 ❈ To scare away birds and other animal from the fields.

Index